I0468928

The Wild Side Coloring Book

S.A. Knight

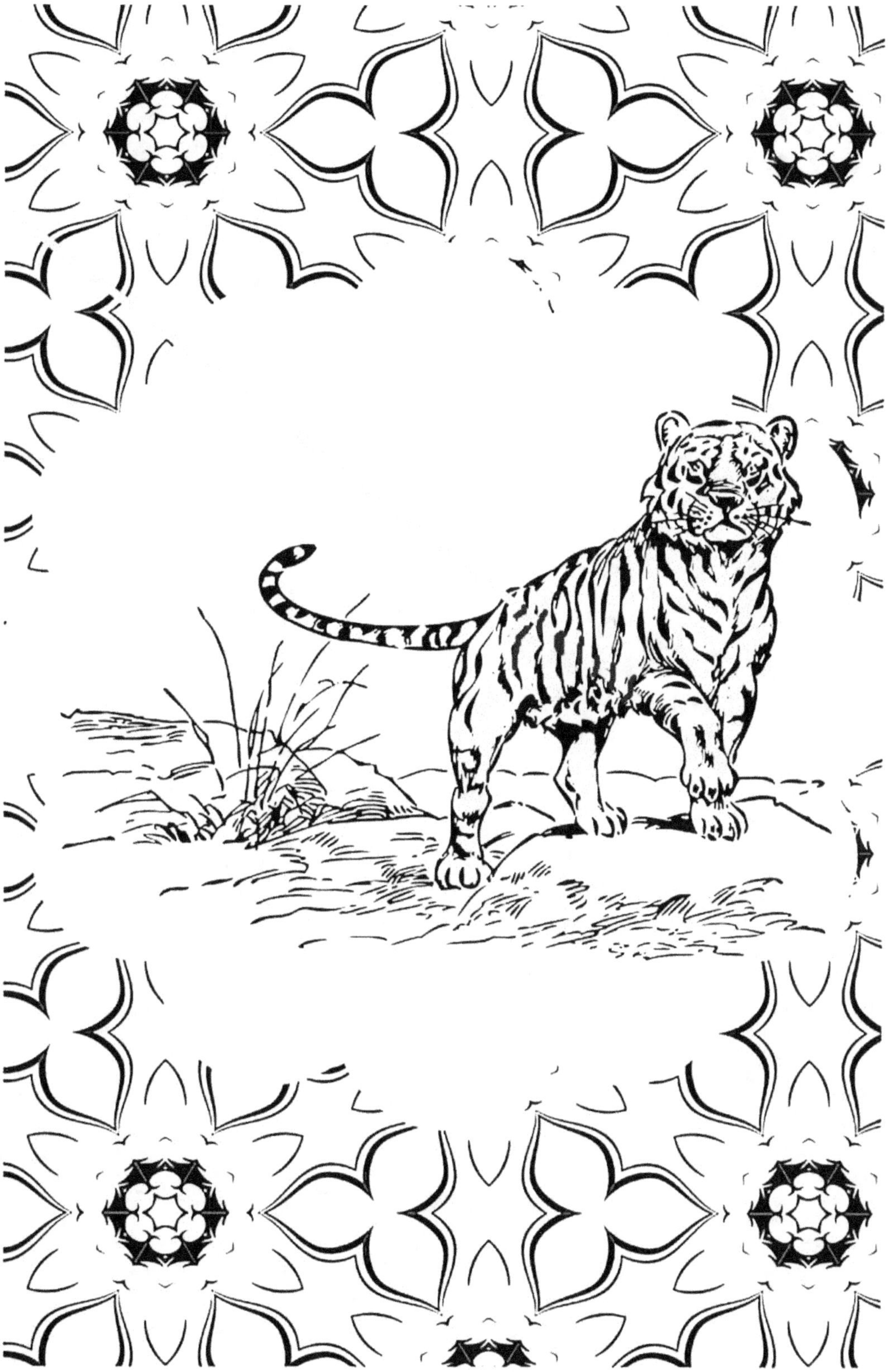

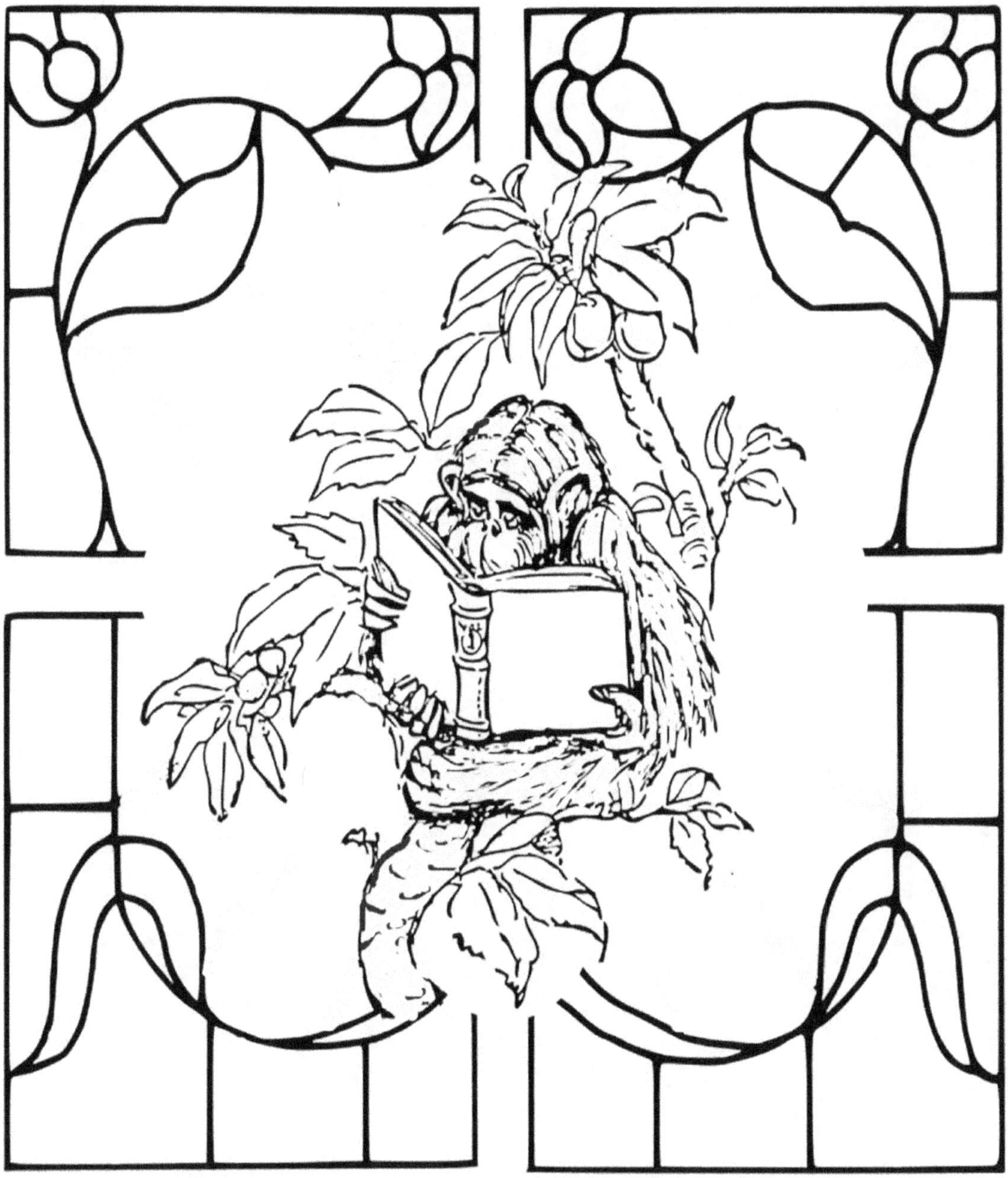

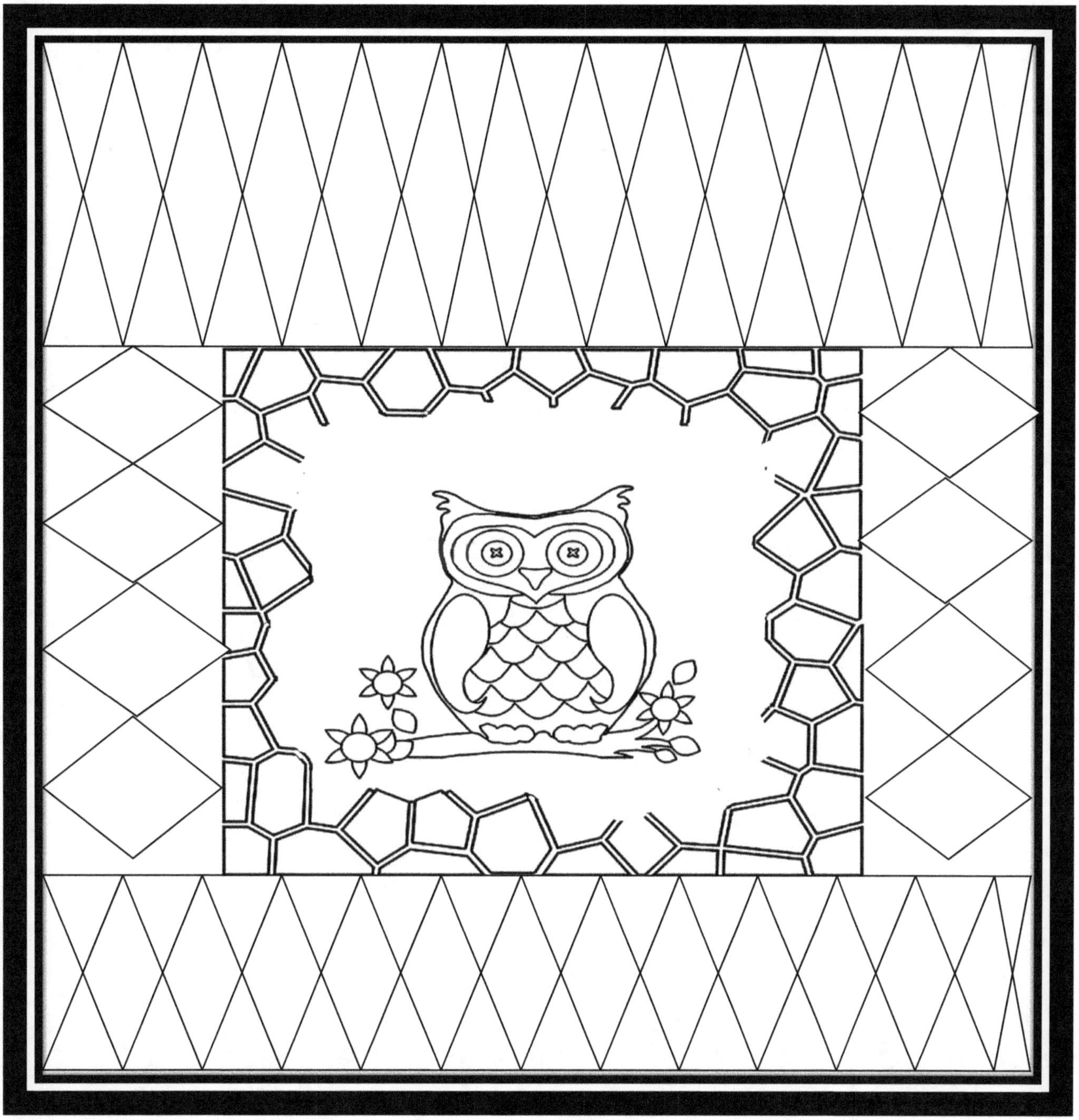

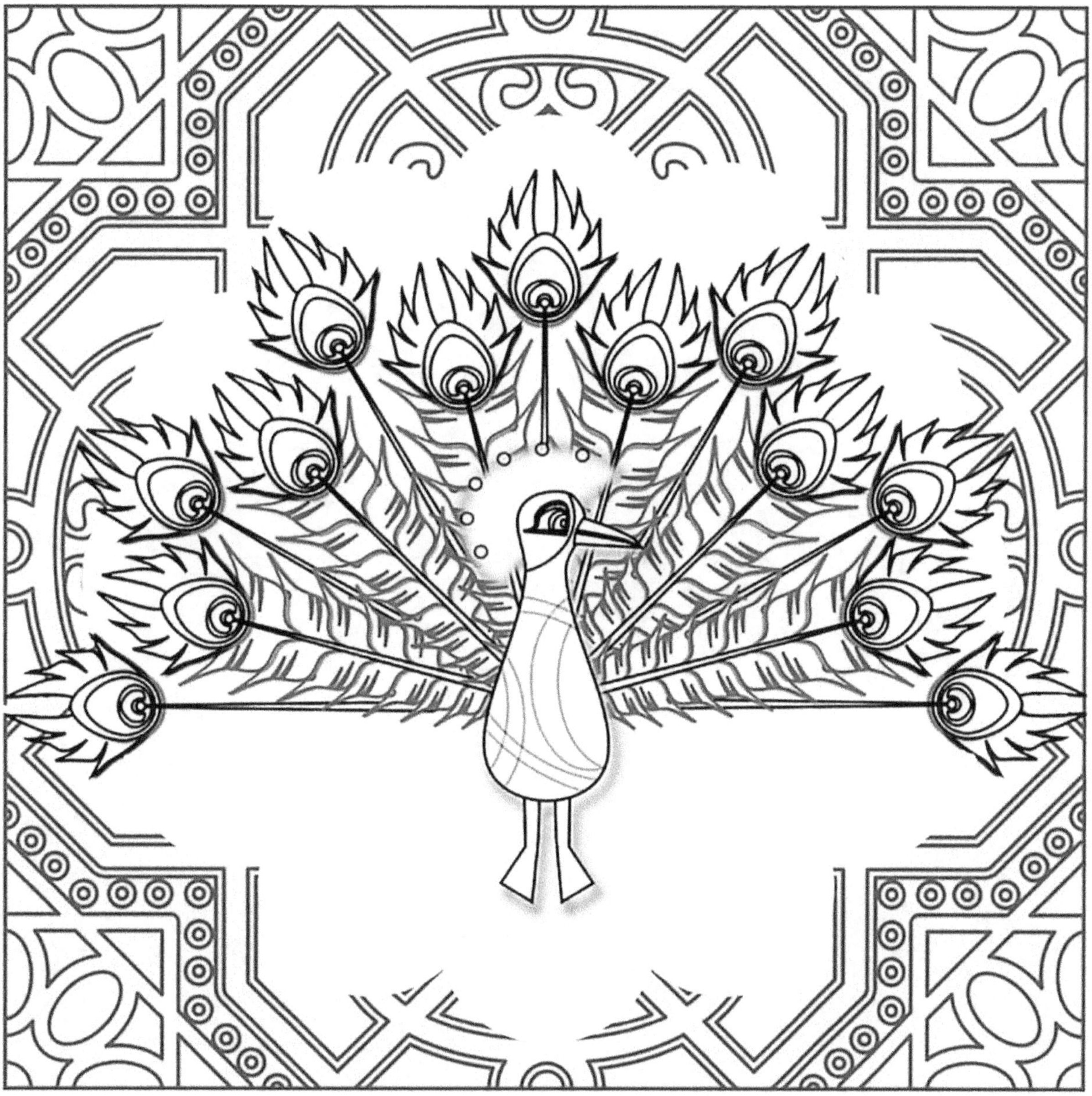

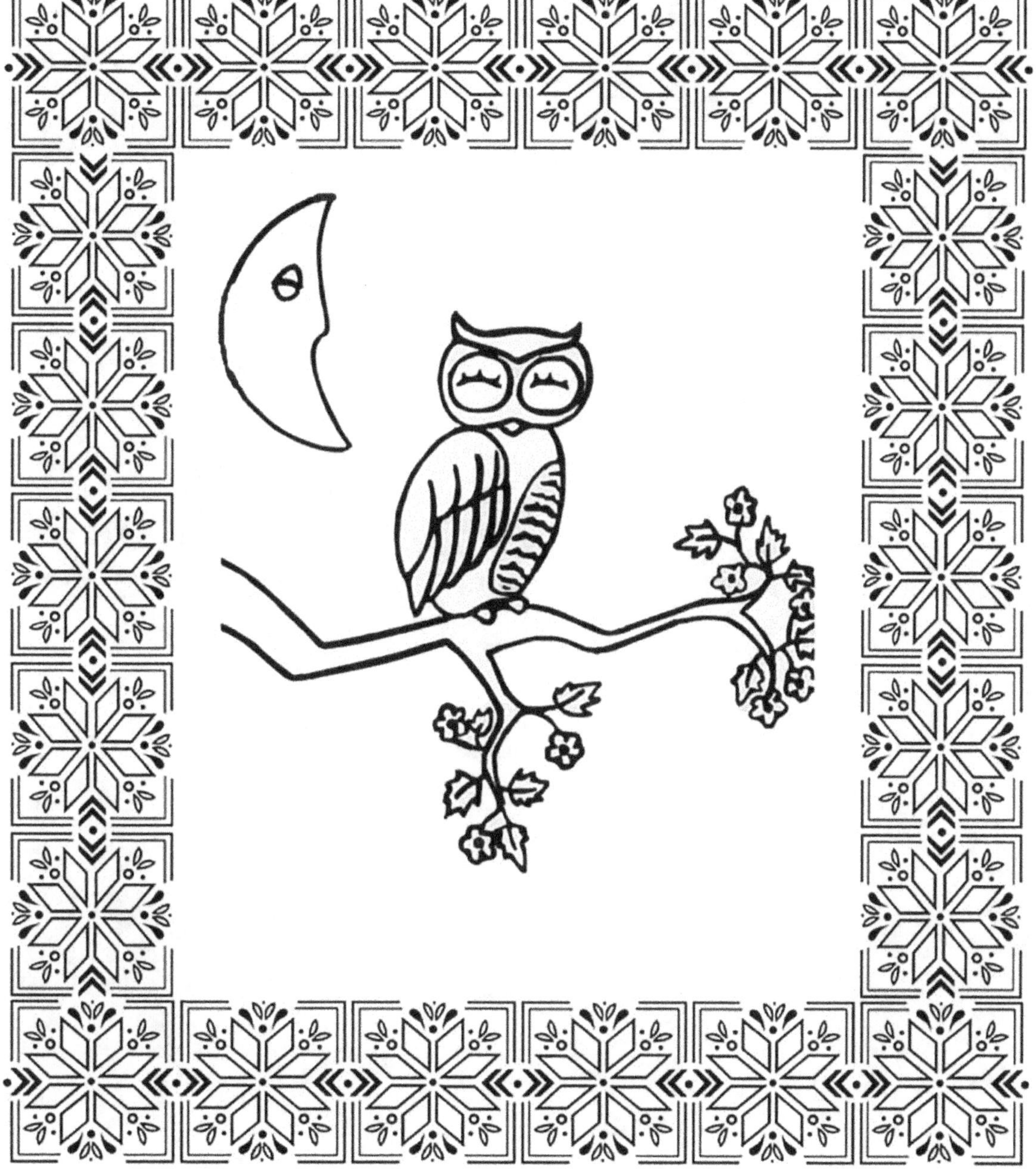

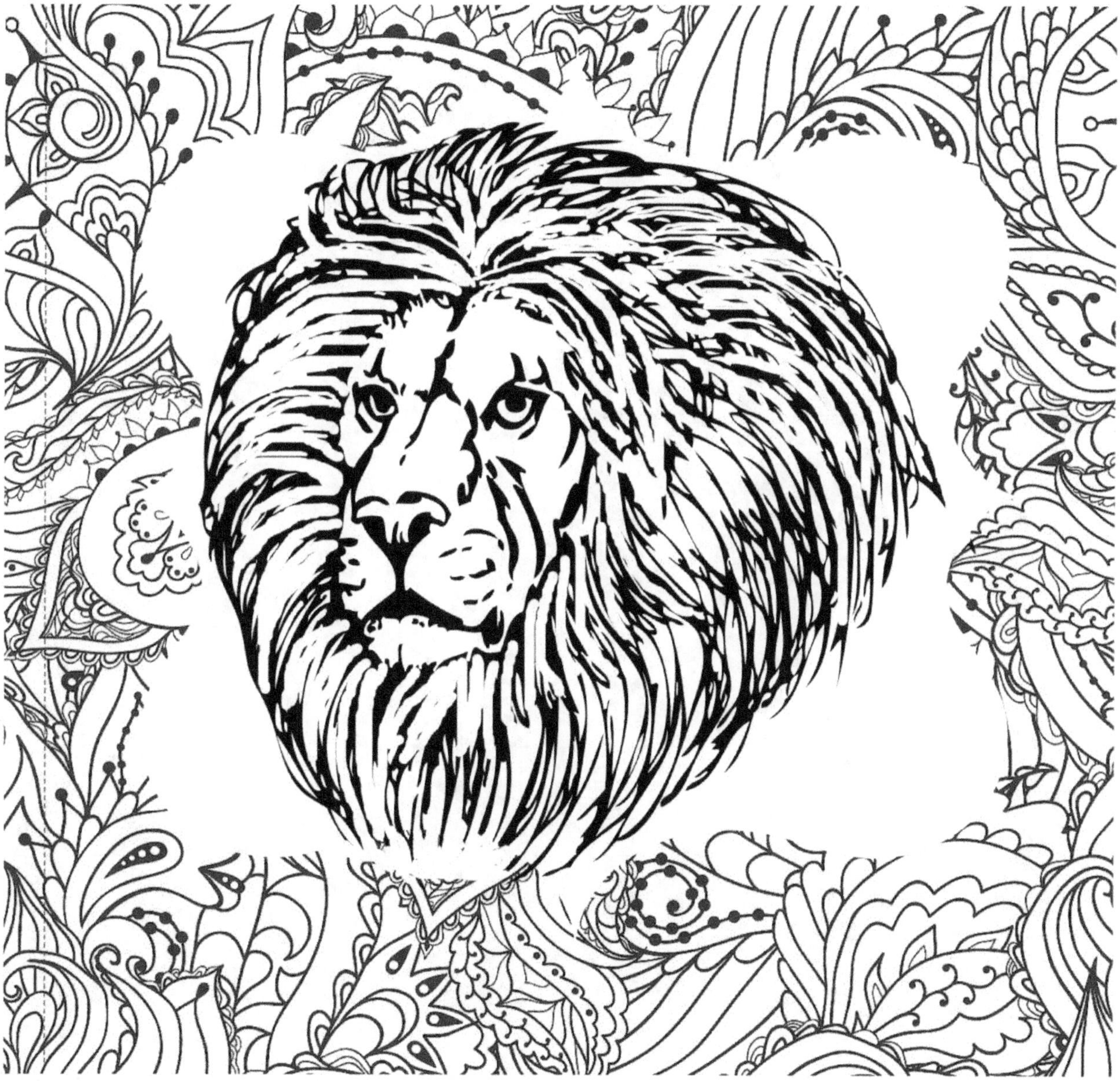

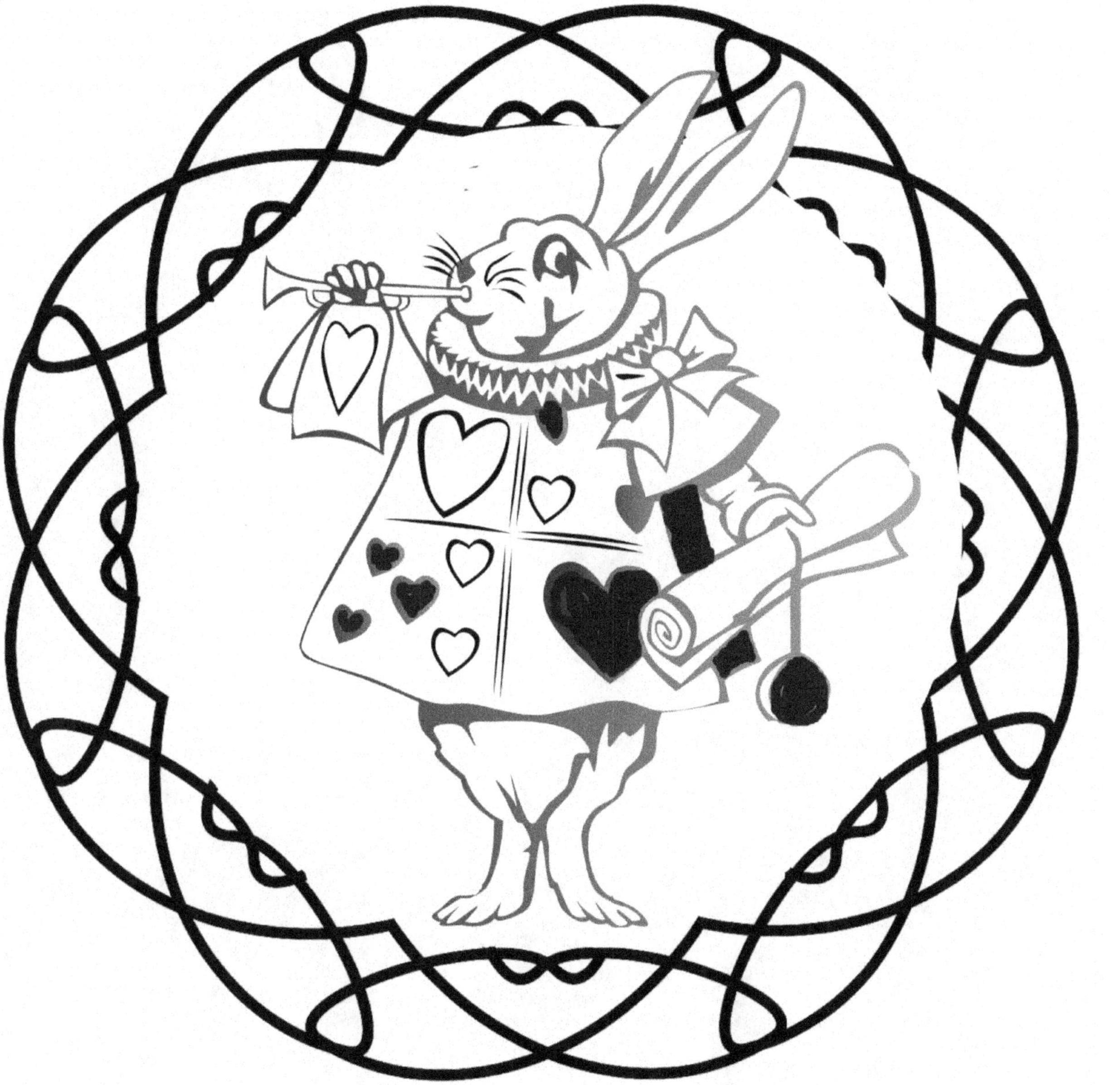

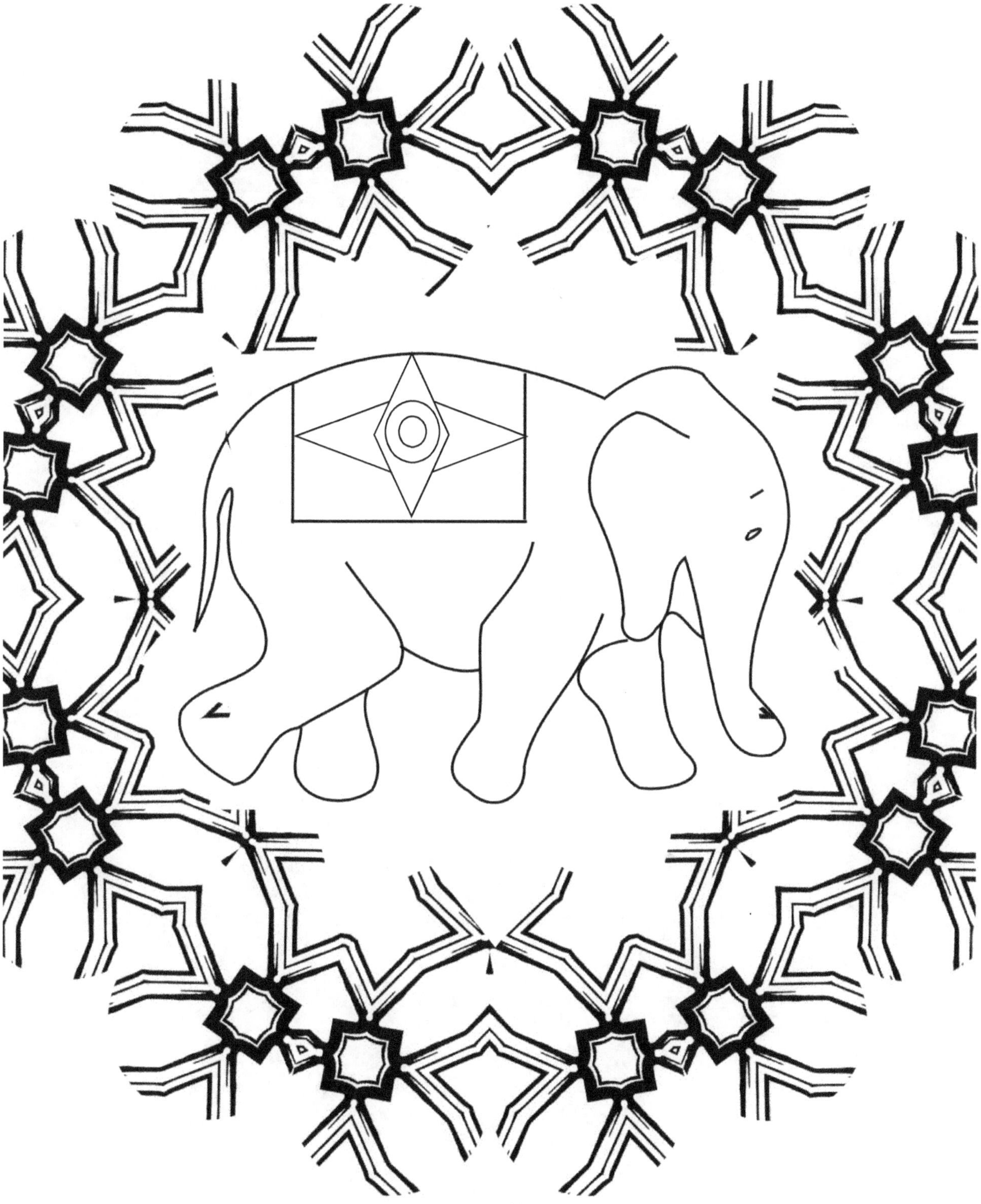

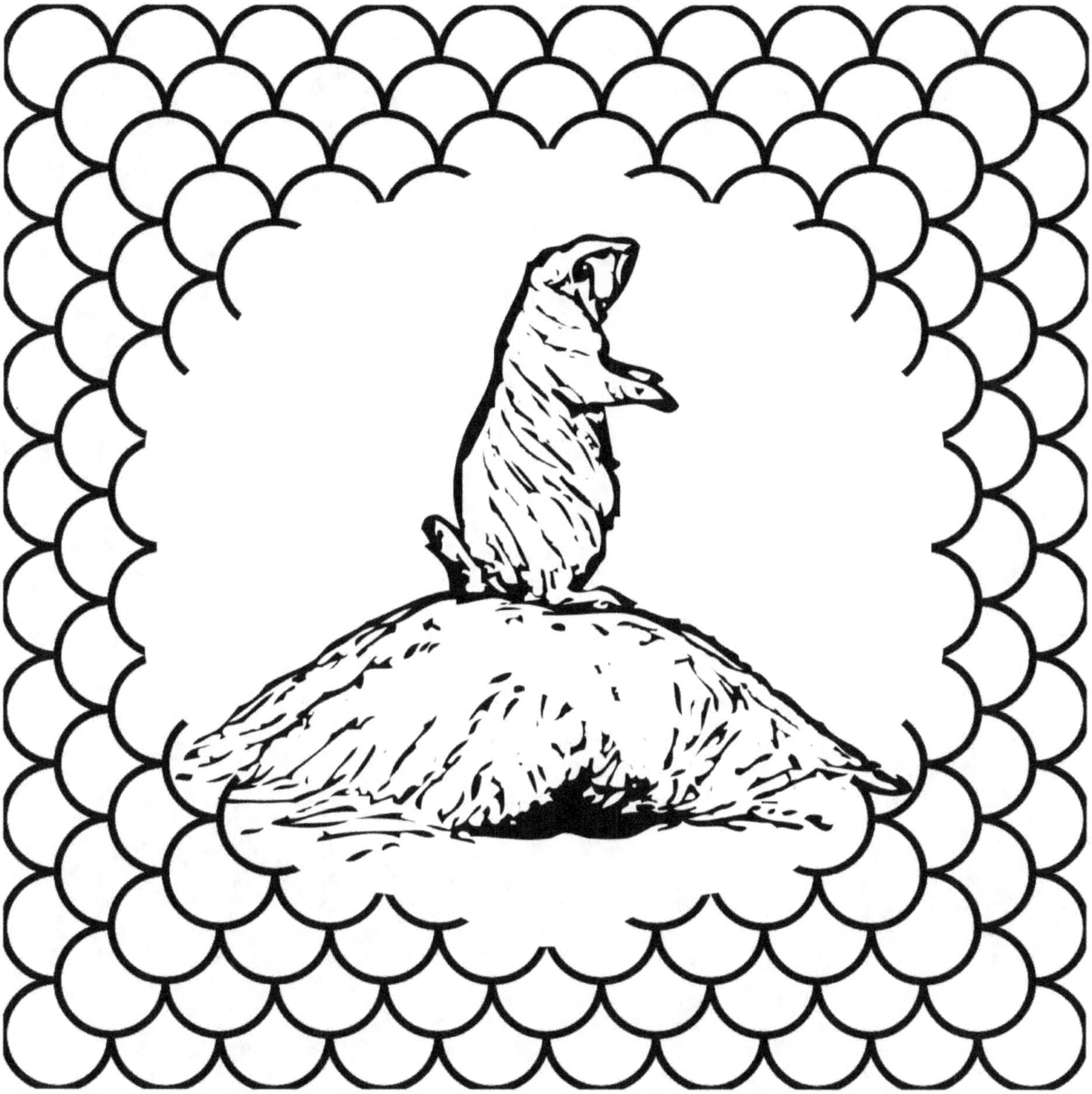

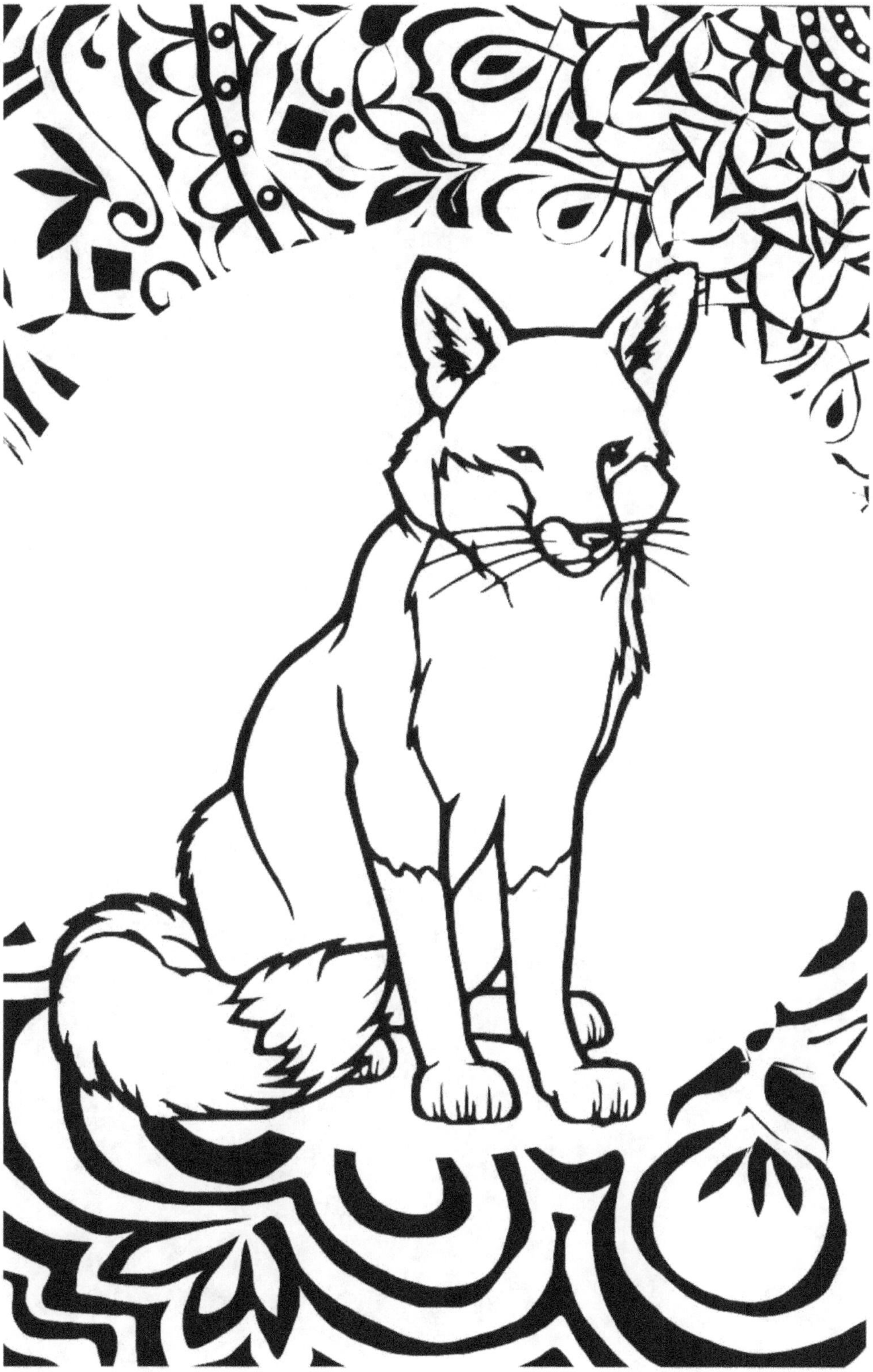

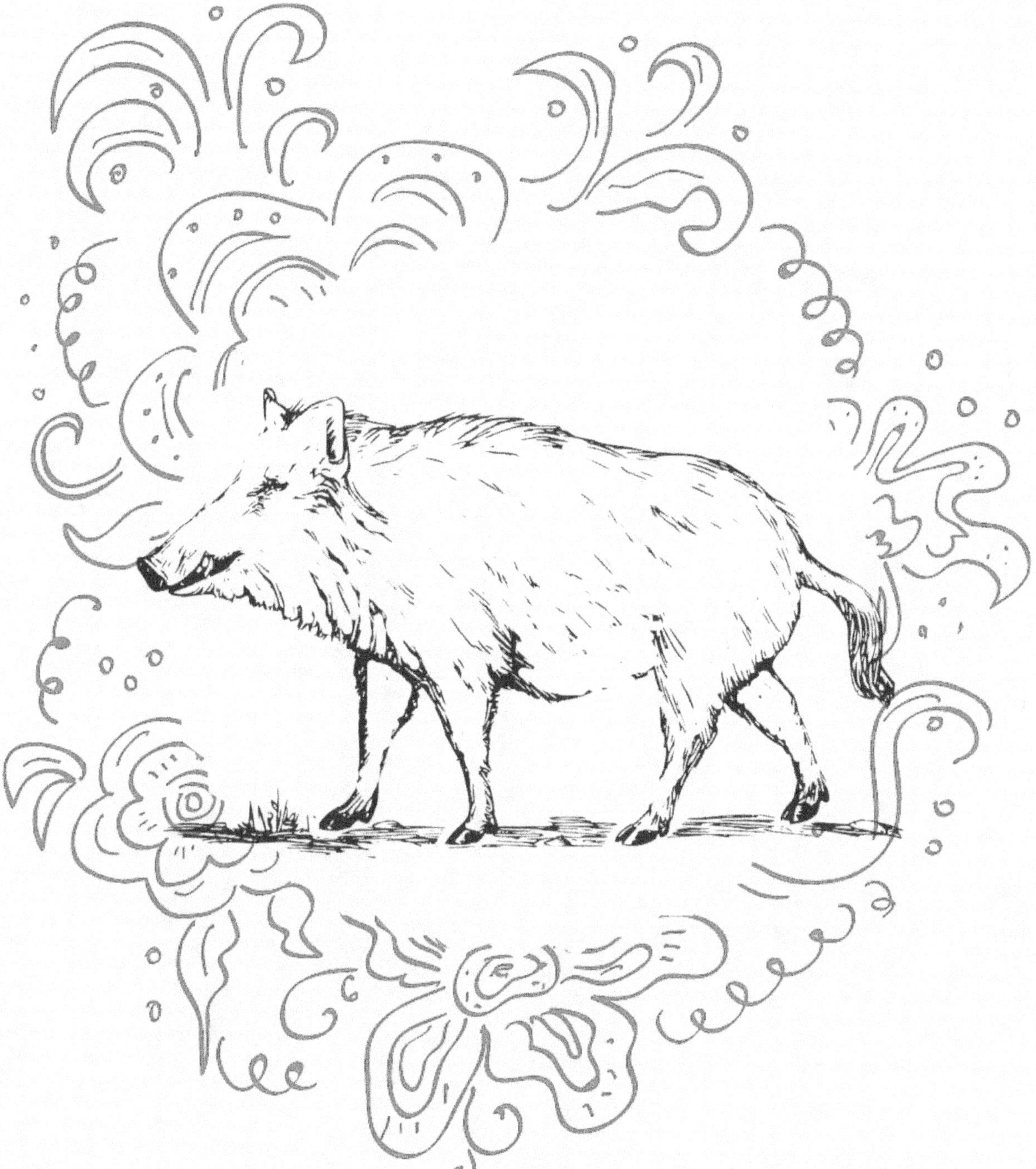

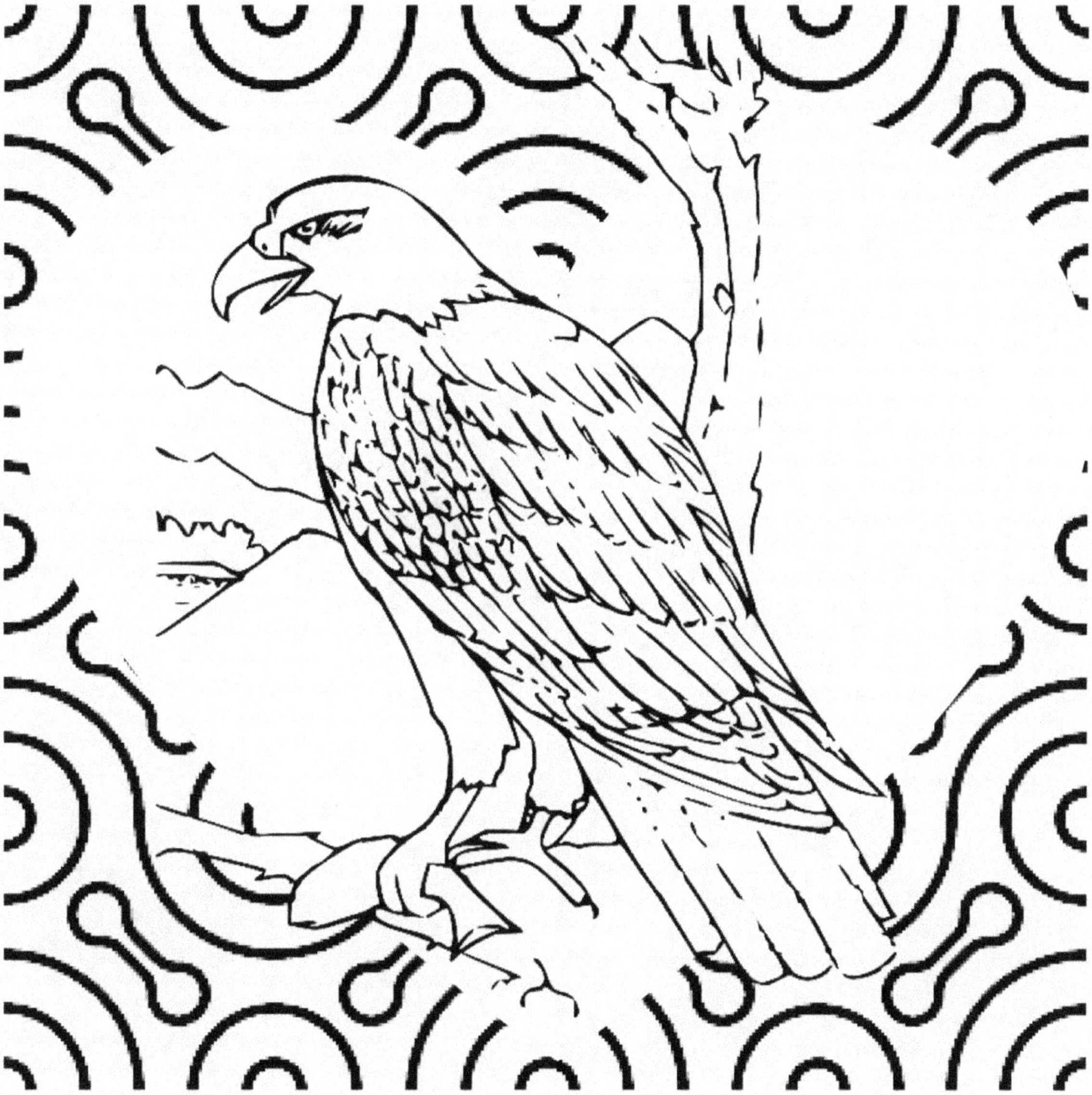

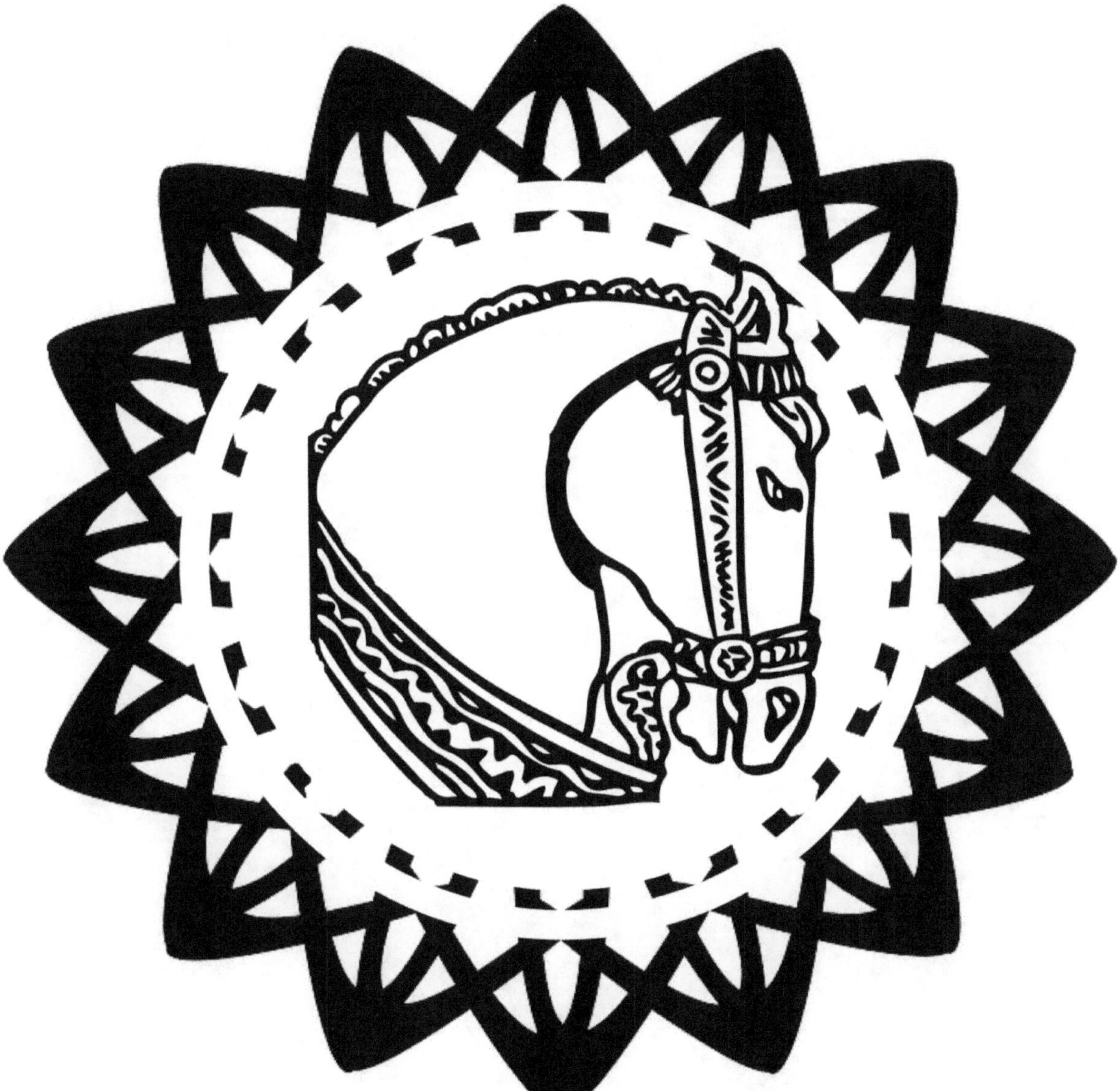

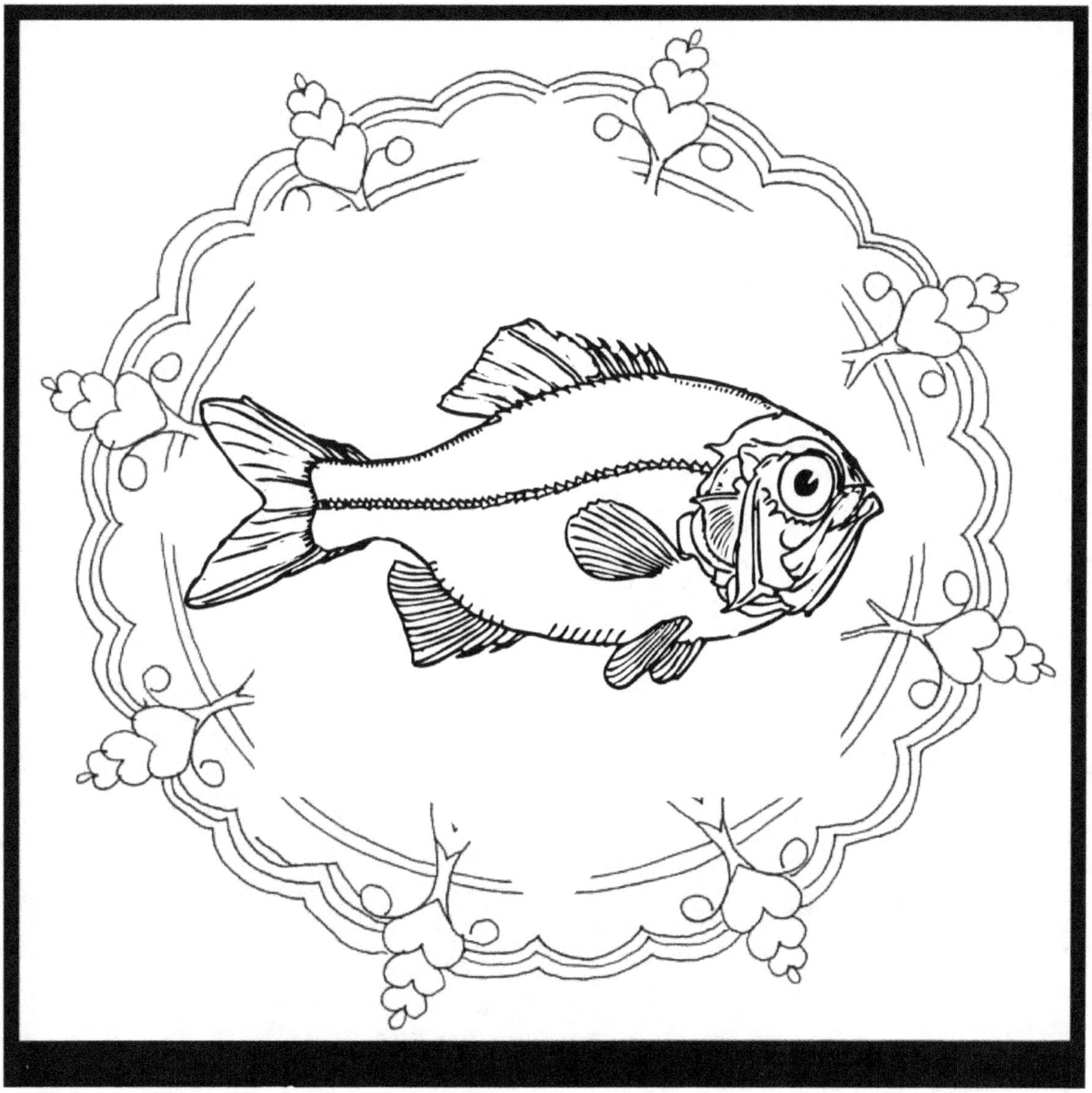

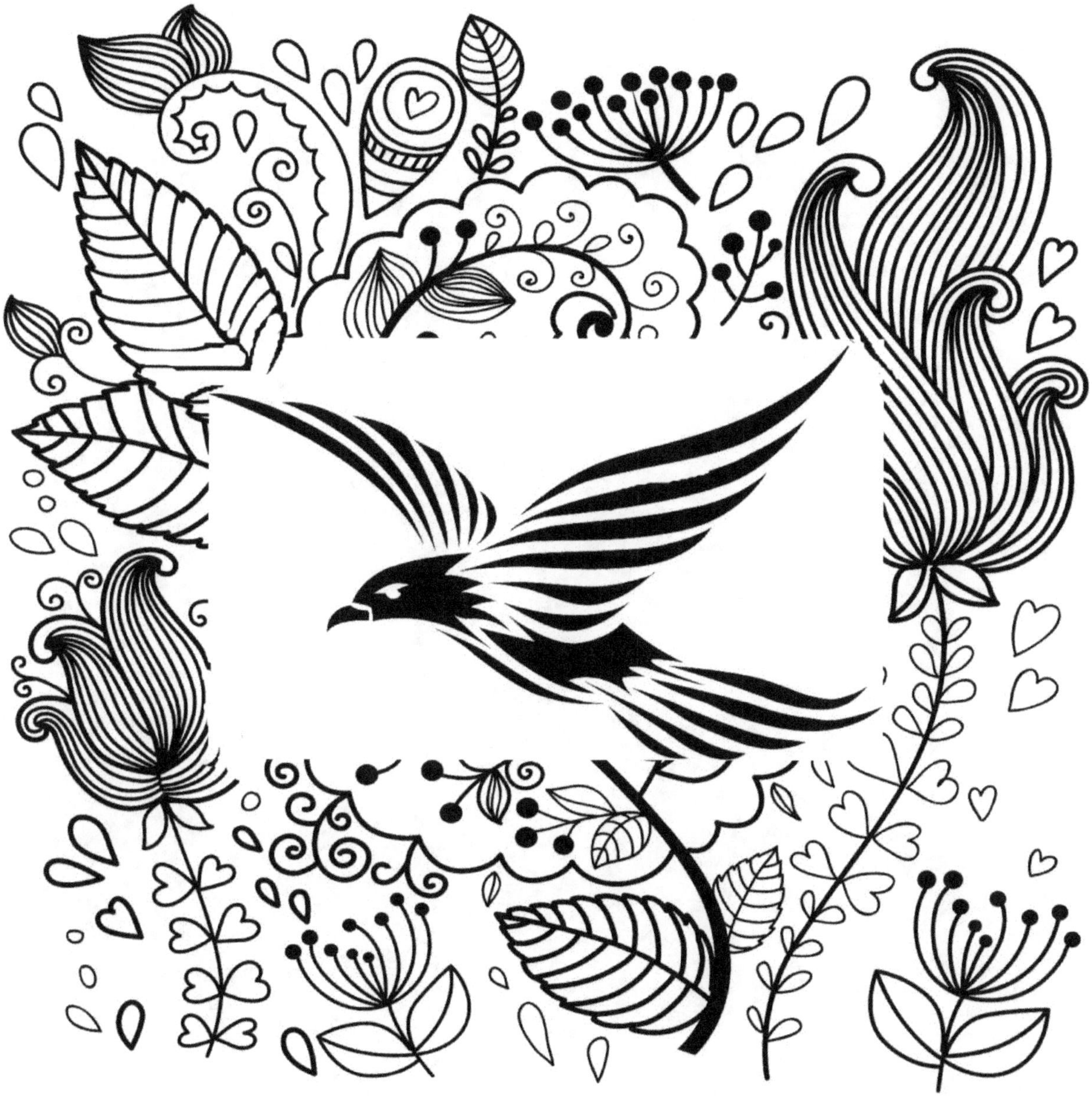

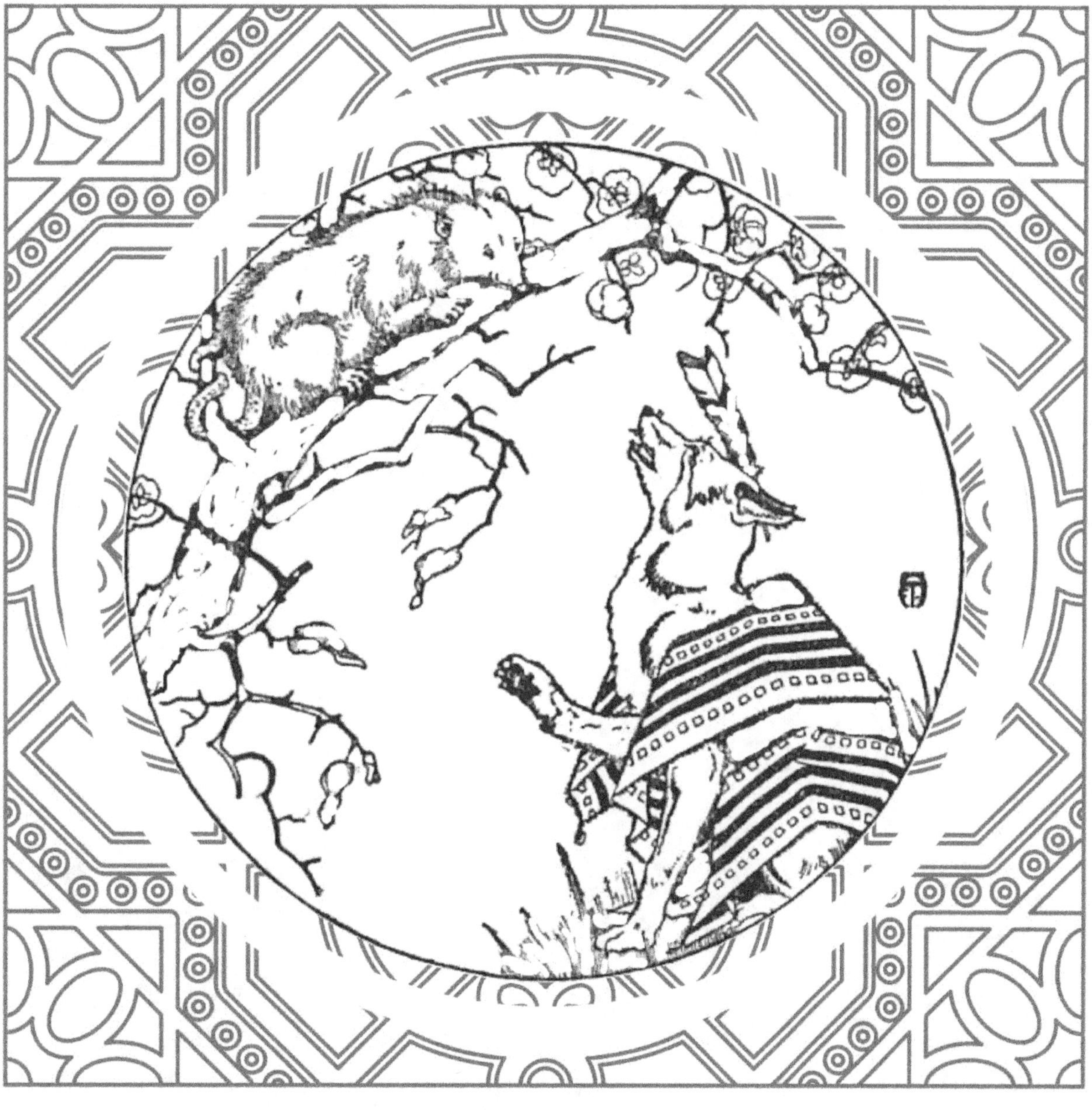

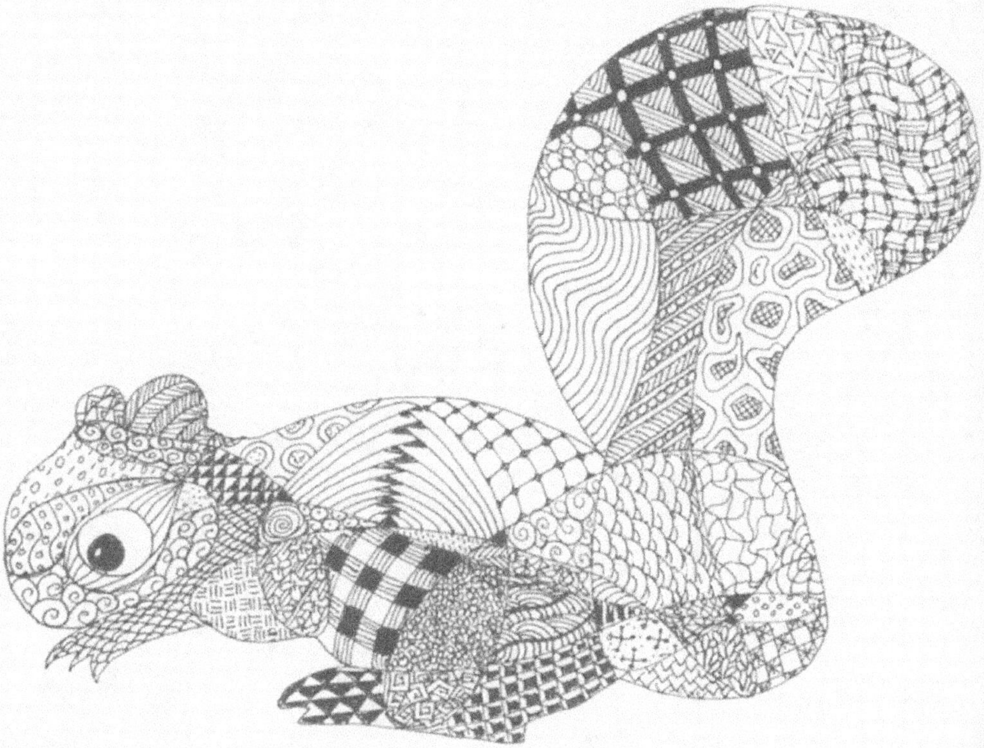

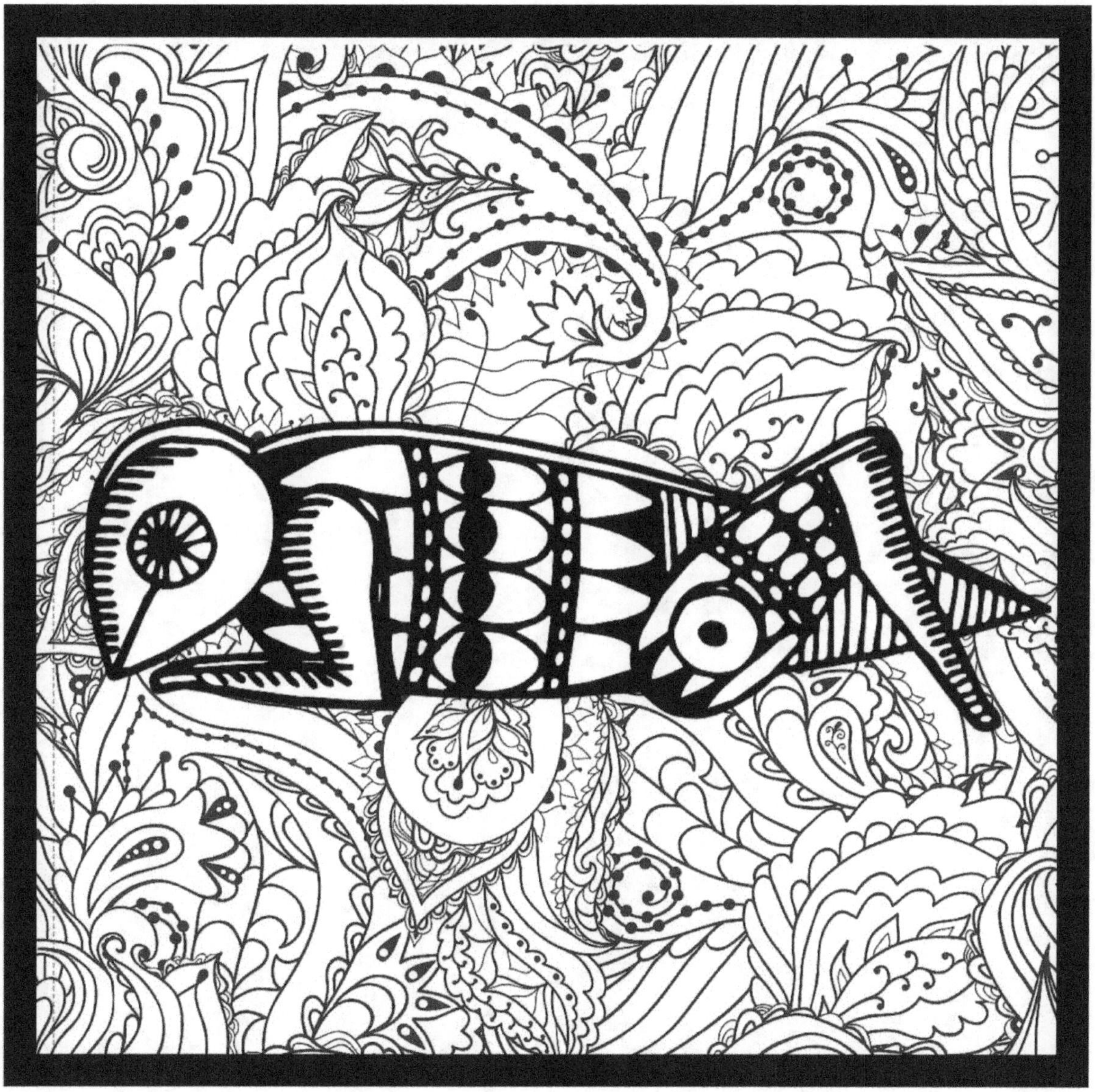

www.ingramcontent.com/pod-product-compliance
Lightning Source LLC
Chambersburg PA
CBHW080524190526
45169CB00008B/3048
* 9 7 8 1 5 3 0 7 9 0 3 8 8 *